Your Own Biggest Cheerleader

By Lachandra B. Baker

To Grandma Millie,

Everything that I am is because of you.

Thank you for being the blueprint that I follow.

Table of Contents

Preface

In a world filled with external pressures dictating who to be, how to act, and what goals to pursue, staying true to our authentic selves becomes a daunting task. The societal mold is so compelling that we often find ourselves either suppressing our true identity to fit in or exaggerating our persona, losing touch with our inner wisdom. This book is both a gentle reminder and a powerful call to action to find that sweet spot where you can wholeheartedly support yourself while lifting others.

Your Own Biggest Cheerleader is a narrative spun together from a diverse range of experiences spanning over five decades of transformation. My story began in the rustic settings of the rural South, where I first encountered the sting of exclusion, and has since taken me through the dynamic realms of corporate boardrooms and the warm, inclusive circles of community gatherings.

- *In these varied spaces, I've advocated for inclusivity, equity, and the undeniable strength of emotional intelligence. Each chapter in this book is a blend of academic insight, real-life stories, and deep introspection, designed to engage your mind, heart, and actions.*

We will explore crucial themes like **self-advocacy, the art of allyship,** the intricacies of **emotional intelligence**, and much more. This isn't just about theories and concepts; it's about practical strategies that can be intertwined into the fabric of your everyday life. To enhance your experience, each chapter concludes with a ***Daily Dose of Pep*** and reflective notes—a personal toolkit for you to absorb, contemplate, and apply these lessons in your life.

Maybe you're picking up this book at a critical crossroads in your life. It could be a career change, a quest to strengthen personal relationships, or a desire to be a more effective advocate for yourself and your community. Regardless of your reason, you're in good company. My story, along with the experiences of others who have walked similar paths, echoes throughout these pages, offering comfort, guidance, and fellowship.

As you delve into each chapter, my hope is that you gain more than just knowledge. I wish for you a transformation of spirit and mindset—not just advice but a validation of your experiences. Most importantly, I hope you find the courage to be your own most passionate supporter, especially in those moments when you feel alone in a vast arena.

Let's set off on our adventure together. *Ready? OK!*

Born to Rebel: A Journey of Self and Defiance

From the earliest days I can remember, I've always been that square peg trying to fit into a round hole. Whether it was the fierce independence that came with being the youngest in my family or simply my nature, I've consistently forged my own path.

I remember a telling incident from kindergarten that exemplifies my rebellious spirit. We were lining up for lunch, and our teacher sternly warned us not to touch the walls. To me, it felt more like a challenge than a rule. Unsurprisingly, my defiance didn't go unnoticed. The result? A trip to the principal's office and a stint at the "bad kid's table" in the cafeteria. The stares and whispers from my classmates were a heavy burden for such a small act of rebellion. Looking back, the public shaming seems like a harsh response to a child's harmless defiance.

That episode was a microcosm of the broader challenges I faced growing up as a young Black girl in Sylvania, Georgia, during the '70s and '80s. Society's norms were never constraints for me; they were obstacles to be conquered. My mother, my older sister, and my grandmother's inspiring presence all contributed to the development of my resilience at home. My grandmother, in particular, was a font of wisdom, constantly urging me to value my uniqueness and to challenge the norms.

My early school years presented their own battles. Academically, I excelled, but I often found myself in conflict with a curriculum that lacked representation. I wasn't one to passively accept this. I questioned, I challenged, and I sought out the rich history and literature of African American culture, going beyond what was taught in the classroom.

Adolescence brought its own set of trials. The search for identity during those years was fraught with self-doubt and uncertainty. Yet, with each challenge, I learned to embrace my individuality more fiercely, refusing to conform to societal expectations. Reflecting on these experiences, it's evident how each act of defiance and each challenge molded me into who I am today. They strengthened my resolve, teaching me the value of perseverance and authenticity. I've realized that the essence of a fulfilling life is staying true to oneself.

I've become my own strongest advocate, embracing my identity and standing up for myself. By facing challenges head-on, I've blazed my own trail. My aim is to inspire others to embrace their true selves and chart their own paths by sharing my story.

In the upcoming chapters, I'll explore key moments of resilience and victory that have defined my experience. I believe that embracing our true selves and chasing our dreams allows us to lead lives filled with joy, purpose, and self-love.

Life is full of defining moments and crossroads that challenge our identity. I've faced many such junctures, whether they were significant life changes or personal revelations. These moments compel us to reflect on who we are and what we truly desire.

Embarking on a journey of self-discovery is crucial to fully understanding and accepting oneself. While it can be daunting, it's invariably illuminating. It's about recognizing and celebrating our uniqueness and understanding that our flaws add richness to our character.

As we travel down this road together, it's important to approach it with compassion and self-love. Self-reflection is not about self-criticism; it's about growth, understanding, and acceptance. Embracing every aspect of ourselves paves the way for bona fide self-love and personal evolution.

Introduction: The Catalyst for Change: Why This Book Matters to Me and to You

My life has been a transformative exploration, stretching far beyond the confines of my hometown. Through travel and exposure to diverse cultures and perspectives, I've come to understand the immense potential each of us holds. We can break free from societal norms and wholeheartedly embrace our true selves. In a world that often tries to diminish us and hinder our aspirations, we must summon the strength within to surmount these challenges and become our greatest supporters.

This book describes an extraordinary path that was filled with tenacity, triumph, and unwavering self-advocacy. It is my story. Rising up against all odds, I overcame prejudice, poverty, and self-doubt.

As the author, I stand before you as a champion of individuality and freedom. In the pages that follow, I aim to share my experiences, triumphs, and the invaluable lessons learned along the way. This narrative is more than a personal account; it's a testament to the power of self-belief, authenticity, and the relentless pursuit of a life free from fear and harm to oneself and others.

This book celebrates the resilience of the human spirit, offering a beacon of hope that regardless of our circumstances or challenges, there's an inner resilience that can guide us through the darkest times. My hope is that my story will inspire you to find the courage, strength, and determination to be your own greatest advocate.

Within these pages, you'll find uplifting stories and motivational insights mixed together, serving as a reminder of your inherent worth and the boundless opportunities that await. I firmly believe that we all deserve a life where we can shine brightly, unencumbered by the limitations imposed by others. We'll explore the transformative power of self-advocacy and the importance of nurturing our dreams, no matter how audacious they may seem. Delving into personal growth, we'll uncover the skills and strategies necessary to embrace our authenticity and craft a life aligned with our deepest desires.

Open your heart and mind to the transformative possibilities within. Together, let's celebrate the spirit of self-advocacy, embracing our differences, and striving for a world free of fear and discrimination. If these words have reached you, it's not coincidental. I believe wholeheartedly in your potential and your power. You're not alone. I'm in your corner, cheering you on passionately. As you turn these pages, my deepest hope is that you uncover the wisdom, motivation, and courage to champion yourself and others, becoming an advocate for a world where every voice matters, every dream is valid, and every person is celebrated.

In these words, you'll find more than a guide. You'll find a mentor, a friend, and a reminder that you possess the strength to be your own biggest advocate. Let's embark on this incredible journey of self-discovery, empowerment, and the pursuit of living our truth.

Chapter 1: Be Your Own Hype Person

"When the world is silent, even one voice becomes powerful." — Malala Yousafzai

Leveling Up

My southern upbringing in the early 1970s was vividly marked by unpaved roads, addresses that seemed like cryptic codes, and the looming, ominous shadow of the Ku Klux Klan. Their actions had a profoundly negative impact on my family, particularly shaping my grandmother's life and molding her into a figure of immense resilience. This resilience, born out of adversity, became a legacy that she passed down through generations.

I grew up under the care of my mother and grandmother, without the presence of my father. His absence created a significant void in my life, influencing my early years and my future relationships in ways I'm still unraveling. Over time, I've learned to understand and even appreciate the choices my mother made under those circumstances. Our neighborhood was predominantly Black, with only one other White family nearby. My racial identity has always been a significant part of who I am, presenting its own set of challenges and moments for pride.

I gained a distinct perspective on life from having two strong women of different generations raise me. The experiences I had, both the good and the challenging, have deeply influenced how I respond to life's various situations. No matter what one's childhood looked like—whether it was idyllic or fraught with difficulties—it's crucial to face, understand, and process those early experiences. For some, this might mean introspective reflection; for others, it could involve seeking professional support. There's absolutely no shame in asking for help. We are all part of a larger community, and sometimes we need others to guide and support us.

Self-advocacy is a critical concept in my life. It means standing up for yourself and your interests, especially when it seems like no one else will. It's about being empowered to communicate effectively, make informed decisions, and pursue opportunities that align with your personal goals. This skill has been instrumental in navigating the complexities of my life and has played a significant role in shaping who I am today.

Vibes, Voices, and Victory Moves

Alright, let's delve deep into the transformative world of self-advocacy. Picture this: in the grand narrative of your life, you're not just a passive observer; you're the protagonist, the leading star. And just as every hero needs their own chorus of supporters, you need to be your own most fervent champion. Why, you ask? Well, research indicates that self-advocacy is a linchpin in career progression. But its significance transcends the confines of office spaces and job titles. Embracing and asserting your worth has a ripple effect, bolstering not only your professional trajectory but also fortifying your mental and emotional well-being.

When you muster the courage to articulate your needs and aspirations, clarity becomes your best ally. A well-defined request or assertion eliminates ambiguity, paving the way for more effective communication. The more lucid and precise you are in expressing your needs, the higher the likelihood of them being acknowledged and addressed. But here's the golden nugget: **always anchor yourself in the knowledge of your intrinsic value.** Every individual, ***including you***, brings a distinct blend of skills, perspectives, and experiences to the table. Recognizing and harnessing this uniqueness can be your ace in the hole, especially during negotiations or when differentiating personal and professional boundaries.

Now, self-advocacy isn't a switch you flip on in specific settings; it's a continuous evolution, a mindset. Whether you're presenting a pitch in a boardroom, discussing a project over a casual coffee, or even navigating personal relationships, championing your needs and values is paramount. It's more than just a strategy; it's an odyssey of self-discovery, empowerment, and cultivating a deep-seated respect for oneself. By making these choices, you not only uplift yourself but also set a precedent, inspiring others to recognize and advocate for their worth in various facets of their lives. **You can create your own Victory Moves!** If you need help getting started, below are some helpful techniques, recommendations, and practices you can do to grow your own capacity for effective self-advocacy.

Cheer Technique Breakdown

- **Assertiveness in Career Advancement:** Being assertive is about clearly expressing your needs and standing up for your rights. This skill is often linked to higher job satisfaction and career advancement.

- **Self-Advocacy and Mental Health:** Advocating for oneself can lead to a more balanced work-life equation, reducing stress and enhancing mental well-being.

First Day in the Cheer Spotlight

- **Identify Your Needs:** Make a list of what you need in your professional life.
- **Practice Assertiveness:** Start with small conversations where you express your opinion or needs clearly.

Daily Dose of Pep

1. When was the last time you had to advocate for yourself? How did it make you feel?

2. What are some barriers you face when trying to advocate for yourself?

Confessions of a Cheer Rookie

Reflect on a time when you could have advocated for yourself but chose not to. What held you back? What would you do differently now?

Raise Your PomPoms:

- **Free**: Journal about your experience and what you learned.
- **Extravagant**: Treat yourself to a professional development course to further hone your advocacy skills.

Rally-Up Affirmation

"I am my own advocate, my own voice, my own cheerleader—Go, Me, Go!"

Chapter 2: Allies Assemble!

"In the end, we will remember not the words of our enemies but the silence of our friends." - Martin Luther King, Jr.

Leveling Up

Allyship is the **active, consistent, and ongoing practice of supporting marginalized individuals or groups in the quest for equality and justice**. It goes beyond mere passive support to involve actionable steps that uplift others.

My personal pursuit of allyship has been deeply transformative. During adolescence, I was acutely aware of the barriers faced by people of color, those with disabilities, and marginalized communities. These experiences, though challenging, fueled my resolve to become a force for change in every space I entered. When I became a parent to my LGBTQIA+ children, particularly my youngest, who is transgender and Black, this resolve deepened. Navigating their world alongside them, I learned the true meaning of allyship—**it's not just about support; it's about shared struggles and victories, about understanding their experiences on a profound level.**

This path hasn't been without its hurdles. As a parent, I had to learn, sometimes through trial and error, how to be the best advocate for my child. It involved countless conversations, a lot of listening, and even more learning. There were moments of doubt and fear, but through these experiences I found my strength. I learned the importance of not just speaking for my children but also amplifying their own voices. My role as an ally has been about creating a safe space for them to express themselves, to explore their identity, and to know they are loved and accepted unconditionally.

Reflecting on my career, I recognize the allies who've played pivotal roles in my life. They've come from all walks of life, including White men and women, who've stood by me, challenged me, and pushed me towards my goals. These allies—some unexpected—have shown me that support often comes in diverse forms. They've taught me the importance of empathy, understanding, and collective effort in lifting each other up. This tapestry of experiences and relationships has not only shaped who I am but also how I approach my work, always striving to foster inclusive environments where everyone can find their voice and reach their full potential.

Vibes, Voices, and Victory Moves

Being an ally is not a mere label one can casually adopt; it's a profound commitment to being empathetic, understanding, and proactive in your support. It's about immersing oneself in the lived experiences of the groups you aim to stand beside, ensuring your advocacy is rooted in genuine understanding. Delving into the intricacies of the challenges faced by these communities enriches your perspective, making your support more impactful. However, it's crucial to recognize that knowledge, while foundational, is just the starting point. **An ally doesn't merely accumulate information; they act on it.** Think of allyship as an active endeavor rather than a passive noun. It involves championing causes, challenging prejudices, and, at times, consciously stepping back to let marginalized voices take center stage.

Recent research underscores the criticality of authentic allyship, particularly in professional settings. While many straight, cisgender individuals might self-identify as allies to the LGBTQIA+ community, the litmus test lies in the perceptions of the LGBTQIA+ individuals themselves. **Do *they* view these proclaimed allies as true champions of their rights?** A comprehensive study spanning four years unveiled a disconcerting reality: workplace discrimination and feelings of exclusion remain persistent hurdles for numerous LGBTQIA+ employees. A telling 2018 survey by the **Human Rights Campaign Foundation** *(Campaign, n.d.)* disclosed that nearly half (46%) of LGBTQIA+ employees felt compelled to conceal their true identities in their professional environments. Moreover, a significant 20% sought alternative employment due to an inhospitable workplace culture. These statistics underscore the chasm between performative allyship and positive, impactful support.

But here's the silver lining: Every individual has the capacity to bridge this gap. By continually educating oneself, engaging in open dialogues, and translating knowledge into actionable steps, one can transition from being a passive bystander to an active advocate. Whether your advocacy is geared towards fostering a more inclusive workplace or catalyzing broader societal shifts, the key lies in informed, intentional action. True allyship transcends mere words—it's about standing in solidarity, voicing opposition against inequities, and offering unwavering support with both heart and deed.

Cheer Technique Breakdown

- **Impact of Allyship**: Allyship can help create a culture of inclusion, making marginalized groups feel more welcome and valued. It's not just about 'saying' but 'doing'—taking actionable steps to support others.
- **Active Bystander Intervention**: This involves recognizing a potentially harmful situation and choosing to respond in a way that could positively influence the outcome.

First Day in the Cheer Spotlight:

- **Educate Yourself**: Read up on the experiences of marginalized groups.

- **Speak Up**: Use your privilege to address inequity when you see it.

Daily Dose of Pep

1. Describe an instance where you acted as an ally. What did you learn from that experience?

2. What are some common misconceptions about being an ally?

Confessions of a Cheer Rookie

Reflect on becoming an ally. What are the challenges you've faced, and how have you overcome them?

Raise Your PomPoms:

- **Free**: Share your allyship goals on social media to inspire others.

- **Extravagant**: Donate to a cause that supports marginalized communities.

Rally-Up Affirmation

"Be the ally you wish to see—let's lift others as we rise!"

Chapter 3: A Seat at the Table

"To be an activist is to speak. To be an advocate is to listen. Society can't move forward without both." — Eva Lewis

Leveling Up

Inclusion and **equity** go beyond just opening doors; **they're about ensuring everyone has a seat at the table and a voice in the conversation.** While diversity is about variety, inclusion is about active engagement, and equity is about fairness.

My entire life has been about discovering where I truly belong. From a young age, the importance of academics was deeply ingrained in me by my grandmother. She was forced out of school to work in the cotton fields, missing out on her own educational opportunities. Therefore, she was determined to ensure that my sister and I focused on our education. But despite my academic success, I frequently felt inferior because of my body image. Being a heavier-set, chunky little girl seemed to overshadow my achievements.

Adding to this complexity, in the late '70s and early '80s, my academic achievements led others to label me as a 'white girl,' a hurtful stereotype that equated intelligence with whiteness. This label alienated me from both the Black and White communities in the Deep South city where I grew up. I was constantly torn and trying to find a balance, wondering where I should show up and where I could truly belong.

My path through the complexity of student government served as both a tribute and a test to the principles of self-advocacy. During my time as president of the National Honor Society, Peer Mentors Association, and Student Council in high school, I led by example and lit the way for my college career. During my sophomore year, with the help and encouragement of the student body president from the year before — a visionary lady who thought I had something special — I started a campaign that would put my convictions to the test.

Integrity and the strength of moral principles were the cornerstones of my political strategy. I firmly stood on an actual program, eschewing the all-too-common mudslinging methods. ***"Please vote for me if you agree with my philosophy, but more importantly, please make your voice known."*** The election did not go in my favor, try as I may. A just 46 votes, a tiny fraction of the more than 7,500 voices at our campus, separated me and my opponent, a well-liked linebacker supported by the football team's unity. Only the slim loss was confirmed by a recount.

But after some thought, I realized that what seemed to be a defeat was actually a significant win. During my undergraduate years, my experience was not a diversion but rather a divergence to a route full of possibility and freedom, enabling me to fully immerse myself in pursuits that genuinely connected with my interests and desires. In the meantime, my opponent encountered unanticipated difficulties; his term was characterized by hardships that masked his triumph.

This part of my life serves as a great reminder that perspective may frequently determine how one approaches defeat. Losses can really be wins if they allow us to take additional pathways that are more in line with who we really are. It serves as a reminder that saying "no" to some things in life frequently results in a loud "yes" to others, creating doors to experiences that deepen our growth in unexpected ways.

This lesson is a beacon in the field of self-advocacy, inspiring us to welcome the unanticipated turns in our stories with grace and perseverance because they frequently usher in the most fulfilling periods of our lives.

I made the decision to forge my own path after reading Shirley Chisholm's advice about taking a seat at one's own table. Rather than trying to fit into spaces where I didn't feel authentic, I chose to bring my own folding chair and create my own space at the table. This decision marked a significant turning point in my life. **It became about more than fitting in; it was about finding and asserting my own authentic voice.**

Now, I strive to help others find their sense of belonging, too. For me, it's vital to maintain authenticity and never let anyone diminish it. **Belonging** is more important than merely fitting in. I've learned that **real belonging comes from being true to oneself**, and I'm committed to helping others realize this in their own lives. For me, it's about understanding the importance of self-acceptance and having the courage to embrace one's true self. Everyone deserves a seat at the table, regardless of their background or challenges. I've seen many highs and lows, yet they underscore the significance of self-advocacy and the need for equity in all spheres of life.

Vibes, Voices, and Victory Moves

In our rapidly evolving global landscape, the imperatives of active inclusion and equitable treatment stand out as pillars for sustainable growth and harmony. Let's delve deeper into these concepts. **Active inclusion** isn't just about ticking boxes or meeting quotas; **it's a conscious endeavor to ensure that a rich tapestry of voices, backgrounds, and experiences is not only present but actively engaged and valued.** It's the commitment to ensuring that every individual, irrespective of their background, feels seen, heard, and empowered to contribute. **Equitable treatment**, on the other hand, is **a nuanced understanding that fairness doesn't always equate to uniformity.** It's about discerning the unique needs, challenges, and aspirations of each individual and adapting our approach to ensure that everyone has an equal opportunity to thrive.

McKinsey & Company's research *(Hunt et al., 2018)* has consistently illuminated the direct correlation between organizational diversity and enhanced financial performance. This isn't just a fleeting trend; it's a testament to the tangible benefits that diverse teams bring in terms of creativity, problem-solving, and adaptability. Further amplifying the importance of inclusion is a study from the **Pew Research Center** (*Striking Findings From 2022 | Pew Research Center*, 2022), which revealed that the U.S. population witnessed a surge of 24.5 million between 2010 and 2022 . Intriguingly, Latin American citizens contributed to over half of this growth. Such demographic shifts accentuate the significance of fostering inclusive practices, not just within corporate confines but also in our broader societal fabric.

Organizations that champion the tenets of inclusion and equity are not merely paying lip service to modern ideals. They are strategically positioning themselves to harness the multitude of benefits that come with a diverse workforce, from fostering a culture of mutual respect and collaboration to catalyzing innovation and driving robust financial outcomes. **For professionals at every stage, from seasoned leaders to budding entrants, it's crucial to internalize this: inclusion is far more than a contemporary catchphrase. It's a foundational principle that shapes the future trajectory of businesses and communities alike.** Embracing it wholeheartedly not only enriches our professional endeavors but also elevates our personal interactions, fostering deeper understanding, appreciation, and collaboration in every facet of our lives.

Cheer Technique Breakdown

- **Diversity in Leadership**: Diverse leadership brings varied perspectives, leading to more innovative solutions. It also sets a precedent for lower-level employees, showing that there is room for everyone at the top.
- **Inclusion and Productivity**: An inclusive environment fosters a sense of belonging, which can significantly boost employee engagement and productivity.

First Day in the Cheer Spotlight:

- **Be Inclusive**: Make an effort to include diverse voices in meetings and projects.
- **Challenge the Status Quo**: Question policies that seem to favor one group over another.

Daily Dose of Pep

1. Can you recall a time when you felt truly included? How did that experience impact you?

2. What are some practical steps to promote equity in your daily life?

Confessions of a Cheer Rookie

Think about a situation where you felt excluded or treated unfairly. What could have been done differently to create a more inclusive and equitable environment?

Raise Your PomPoms:

- **Free**: Host a virtual coffee break to celebrate diversity on your team.

- **Extravagant**: Organize a team-building retreat focused on inclusion.

Rally-Up Affirmation

"Inclusion starts with 'I', but it's completed by 'We'—

Together, We Thrive!"

Chapter 4: The Dance of Self-Advocacy: Embracing Emotional Intelligence and Navigating Neurodiversity

"I learned a long time ago the wisest thing I can do is be on my own side, be an advocate for myself and others like me." — Maya Angelou

Leveling Up

Self-advocacy is a delicate interplay of introspection and outreach, a dance between comprehending one's inner emotional landscapes and establishing sincere external connections. At its core, this journey begins with self-awareness—diving deep into our emotional reservoir to discern the ebb and flow of our feelings and their significant influence on our actions and choices. Such introspective processes form **the cornerstone of Emotional Intelligence (EQ)** *(Emotional Intelligence (EQ): Components and Examples, 2024)*, a transformative concept that greatly impacts various life domains.

But the beauty of EQ extends beyond mere self-reflection; it encompasses interpersonal dynamics, fostering connections that are both resonant and enduring. These connections **are birthed from empathetic listening, a principle central to Nonviolent Communication (NVC)** *(Schaefer, 2024).* By listening with our hearts and attuning to underlying emotions and needs, we pave the way for more authentic and fulfilling relationships.

My journey with EQ began as the youngest in a family where I was often labeled as 'dramatic.' This label, seemingly innocuous, deeply influenced my self-perception, leading me to experience emotions with intense volatility. However, the turning point came when I delved into emotional intelligence. **Recognizing and understanding my emotions provided me with a map to navigate previously uncharted emotional territories.** As I honed these skills, not only did my interpersonal relationships transform, but my self-view shifted significantly. No longer seeing myself as merely 'dramatic' or 'extreme,' I recognized a capacity for deep emotional understanding and connection.

Living with undiagnosed ADHD into adulthood added another layer to my journey, presenting a mosaic of challenges often misunderstood by others. This oscillation between highs and lows, coupled with a relentless battle with depression, painted a life in constant flux. **Yet, the journey towards self-recognition and acceptance, aided by counseling and medication, was both arduous and enlightening.** Recognizing that I was not fundamentally flawed but simply different marked a pivotal moment of liberation.

In this journey, my husband emerged as an invaluable ally, dedicating himself to understanding ADHD. His steadiness allowed me the freedom to soar, transforming our relationship into a symbiotic dance of grounding and uplifting. This dynamic partnership became not just a personal triumph but a beacon of hope for others navigating the turbulent waters of ADHD and seeking that anchor in their lives.

This narrative of self-advocacy is not just a reflection of personal trials and triumphs but an uplifting tale for others. It underscores the **profound impact of having a champion who sees beyond the challenges to an individual's full potential**, reminding us that support often arrives in the most unexpected forms. In sharing this chapter of my life, my heartfelt desire is to uplift and inspire, offering solace in the knowledge that champions and cheerleaders exist, sometimes in the most unanticipated ways.

Vibes, Voices, and Victory Moves

Research emanating from esteemed institutions like the **Yale Center for Emotional Intelligence** *(Emotion Science, n.d.)* sheds light on the multifaceted benefits of

EQ. From bolstering academic achievements and honing leadership acumen to enhancing overall well-being, the positive ripple effects of emotional intelligence are manifold. Furthermore, the symbiotic relationship between EQ and professional success is well documented. Techniques such as NVC emerge as powerful tools in this context, especially when engaging with the complex terrains of conflict resolution and team dynamics.

So, as we navigate the intricate tapestry of life, let's champion the **dual pillars of self-awareness and empathy**. By doing so, we're not merely standing up for our individual needs and aspirations. We're also laying the foundation for a more compassionate, understanding world. A world where emotions aren't just acknowledged but celebrated, where interactions are not transactional but transformational, and where each one of us, equipped with the tools of self-advocacy, can foster connections that are both deep and meaningful, personally and professionally.

Cheer Technique Breakdown

- **Emotional Intelligence and Career**: High EQ often correlates with better team collaboration, effective conflict resolution, and overall career success.
- **NVC and Conflict Resolution**: Nonviolent Communication can be a game-changer in resolving conflicts as it focuses on understanding and collaboration rather than confrontation.

First Day in the Cheer Spotlight:

- **Self-Assessment**: Take an EQ quiz to understand your emotional intelligence level.
- **Active Listening**: Practice listening without interrupting or immediately offering solutions.

Daily Dose of Pep

1. Can you recall an instance where being emotionally intelligent helped you in a tough situation?

2. What are some challenges you've faced while trying to implement nonviolent communication?

Confessions of a Cheer Rookie

Reflect on how EQ shows up for you. Are there specific areas where you feel you could improve? What steps could you take to do so?

Raise Your PomPoms:

- **Free**: Reflect on a recent situation where you successfully applied emotional intelligence.

- **Extravagant**: Enroll in an advanced Emotional Intelligence course.

Rally-Up Affirmation

"Heads up, hearts open—emotionally intelligent, forever evolving!"

Chapter 5: Confidence and The Comeback Kid

"I don't need easy. I just need possible." — Bethany Hamilton

Leveling Up

Self-advocacy, at its essence, is about understanding and embracing the dual forces of confidence and resilience. Confidence isn't just believing in your abilities; it's about rebounding when challenges arise. Resilience is what sustains confidence, helping us navigate the setbacks to achieve long-term success.

My high school years showcased this dance of triumphs and trials. Academically, I soared, securing leadership roles and accolades, including back-to-back regional titles in Extemporaneous Speaking and graduating fourth in my class. Yet, despite these public achievements, my personal struggles painted a contrasting picture. Labeled the "fat girl," I endured cruel taunts that marred my self-esteem, even though, in reality, I was a tall, curvaceous young woman. This misperception, combined with inherent shyness, made my early years daunting.

A turning point arrived during my sophomore year, inspired by the poise of Vanessa Williams, the first Black Miss America. Participating in a lip sync event, I stepped onto the stage with trepidation but left it with a roar of applause and a new-found confidence. Winning the contest was transformative; I was no longer just "Audra's little sister." **I had begun to carve out my own identity, learning the power of self-belief and the importance of embracing my authentic self.**

This journey of self-perception and body image was fraught with challenges. From infancy to adulthood, I grappled with the weight of external criticisms and internal conflicts, which significantly impacted my relationship with my body and self-worth. The decision to undergo bariatric surgery was not taken lightly; it was a dramatic, empowering act of self-advocacy. Losing 112 pounds was both a physical transformation and a reclaiming of control over my life and health.

My post-surgery rebirth was profound. Liberated from the constraints that had long defined my existence, I discovered joy in movement and style—embracing opportunities that had previously seemed out of reach. This experience solidified my appreciation for my intellectual contributions and allowed me to truly embrace my physical self.

This metamorphosis underlines **the power of individual agency and the importance of acting according to one's own needs, irrespective of others' opinions.** It exemplifies a universal truth: everyone's path to self-advocacy and personal fulfillment is unique. What matters most is discovering what works for you, trusting in your choices, and understanding that your own well-being and happiness define your success.

I share my story not as a prescription, but to inspire you to reflect on what it means to stand up for yourself in the most personal aspects of life. Whether embracing oneself as you are or embarking on a transformative journey, the ultimate achievement is being confident in your own skin. Self-advocacy begins with making choices that enhance our happiness and well-being, courageously speaking our truth, and accepting who we are.

Vibes, Voices, and Victory Moves

Confidence and resilience are indeed the twin pillars that uphold the edifice of personal growth and development. Think of them as the yin and yang, each complementing and amplifying the other's strengths. Let's delve deeper into this synergy.

Starting with confidence, it's that unwavering flame within, fueled by self-belief. It's the voice that, amidst the cacophony of doubts and naysayers, resolutely declares, "I can and I will." This self-assurance stems from a profound recognition of one's capabilities, talents, and worth. It's not about arrogance or hubris, but a grounded and honest belief in one's potential. This inner conviction becomes the compass that guides you, especially when navigating uncharted territories or facing daunting challenges.

Transitioning to resilience, it's like the elasticity of a rubber band. Life, with its endless twists and turns, often stretches us to our limits. There are moments of triumph, but there are also phases of setbacks, disappointments, and heartbreaks. Resilience is that intrinsic quality that allows us to stretch, adapt, and then spring back into shape, no matter how intense the pressure. It's about embracing life's adversities, learning from them, and emerging stronger and wiser. Resilience ensures that when confidence wavers, it's not extinguished; it's reignited and restored.

Research published in the **Journal of Positive Psychology** *(Wilson, 2024)* underscores the infinite psychological boons of resilience, highlighting its role in fostering mental fortitude and holistic well-being. Furthermore, insights from the **World Happiness Report** *(Ortiz-Ospina & Roser, 2024)* illuminate the undeniable correlation between self-confidence and life satisfaction. The ripple effects of these attributes extend beyond the personal realm, influencing our professional trajectories, interpersonal relationships, and even our broader societal interactions.

Through the multifaceted tapestry of life, be it charting new career paths, building meaningful relationships, or overcoming personal hurdles, always remember this: **your reservoirs of self-belief and resilience are not just attributes; they're your innate superpowers.** Embrace them, nurture them, and wear them as badges of honor.

Cheer Technique Breakdown

- **Resilience**: Being resilient helps you adapt and bounce back in the face of adversity. It's a skill that can be developed and refined over time.
- **Self-Confidence**: A healthy level of self-confidence can lead to better job performance and overall life satisfaction.

First Day in the Cheer Spotlight:

- **Set Achievable Goals**: Start with small, achievable goals to build your confidence.
- **Celebrate Wins**: No matter how small, celebrate your achievements.

Daily Dose of Pep

1. Describe a time when your confidence was shaken. How did you bounce back?

2. What strategies do you employ to maintain your self-confidence?

Confessions of a Cheer Rookie

Think about a setback you've experienced recently. What lessons did you learn, and how have they contributed to your resilience?

Raise Your PomPoms:

- **Free**: Create a "win wall" where you post your achievements, no matter how small.
- **Extravagant**: Take a weekend getaway to celebrate your newfound confidence.

Rally-Up Affirmation

"I believe in me, especially when I stumble—Bounce Back, Soar Higher!"

Chapter 6: The Support Squad

The only way to succeed is to connect people, share inspiration and support one another." — Deepak Chopra

Leveling Up

Supportive relationships are those that **offer emotional support, mutual respect, and a sense of belonging.** They are essential for personal growth, emotional well-being, and even professional success.

My grandmother, a pillar of strength and wisdom, first woven the threads of perseverance and self-advocacy into the tapestry of my life. I grew up with a single mother who drew strength from my grandmother's well, so I became adept at the complex dance between independence and codependence early on. My mother, a single parent herself, mirrored the resilience of her own upbringing, imparting lessons of self-sufficiency and determination. Yet, beneath the surface of this seemingly self-reliant existence, there lay a deeper truth. A truth that would take years and life's twists to fully understand.

Becoming a single mother was a chapter I never anticipated, yet for six years, it was my reality. In this period, my beliefs about independence, marriage, and gender roles were not just challenged but uprooted. I held onto the notion that to be independent was to be entirely self-sufficient, not needing anyone. This belief was a shield that I thought protected me, but in reality, it kept me from experiencing the full spectrum of human connection and support. It was a lonely path, one that I walked with a mix of pride and hidden longing for companionship and support. Then, life introduced me to my husband, a turning point that reshaped my understanding of interdependence and partnership. In him, I found not just a partner but a mirror reflecting back on the misconceptions I held about marriage and gender roles. Through our union, I learned that **independence**

doesn't mean isolation, and seeking help or guidance isn't a sign of weakness. It's a recognition of our inherent human condition—that **we are social beings, wired for connection and collaboration.** This realization was liberating, underscoring the fact that everyone, regardless of their strength or resilience, needs guidance and grace every day. No one, I learned, can truly navigate the complexities of life alone.

Vibes, Voices, and Victory Moves

Building strong relationships is like sculpting a work of art; it's a delicate blend of time, effort, and real emotion. Every interaction, every shared moment, adds another brushstroke to this evolving masterpiece. Central to this profound process is the art of active listening. It transcends the realm of mere auditory reception; it's about immersing oneself in the essence of what's being conveyed. It's about resonating with the emotions, the unsaid words, and the underlying sentiments. Active listening offers a silent embrace, a gesture that communicates, **"I acknowledge you, I value you, and I'm truly present in this moment with you."**

However, the fabric of partnerships is constructed from mutual strands. It is not a solitary undertaking but rather a collaborative dance in which each step and move is coordinated with the others. This is where the idea of reciprocity shines. True support does not include unilateral giving or taking; rather, it is a peaceful exchange in which both partners uplift and are uplifted in turn. This cyclical flow of energy, caring, and understanding strengthens the relationship, making it more durable and meaningful.

Research emanating from esteemed institutions like the **National Institute of Mental Health** *(Casanova et al., 2022)* underscores the profound impact of social support on our psychological well-being. The feeling of being seen, heard, and valued acts as a protective buffer, enhancing our resilience and overall mental health. Furthermore, the world of academia and professional development reverberates with the significance of mentorship. Numerous studies in professional journals elucidate the transformative role of mentor-mentee relationships in shaping career trajectories, fostering skill development, and opening doors to new opportunities.

No matter what kind of relationships you're navigating in life—the reassuring friendships with loved ones or the illuminating guidance from an experienced mentor—keep in mind that the power of support and mentorship is magical. It can transform problems into opportunities and goals into tangible accomplishments. Every stride, gesture, and shared moment demonstrates the transformational power of authentic connection and mutual progress.

Cheer Technique Breakdown

- **Social Support**: A strong support network can act as a buffer against stress and significantly improve mental well-being.
- **Mentorship**: A good mentor can provide invaluable career advice, open doors to opportunities, and offer emotional support.

First Day in the Cheer Spotlight:

- **Reach Out**: Don't be afraid to ask for help or offer it.
- **Find a Mentor**: Look for someone who has walked the path you're embarking on.

Daily Dose of Pep

1. Who are the people in your "Support Squad," and how have they impacted your life?

2. How do you contribute to creating supportive relationships in your circles?

Confessions of a Cheer Rookie

Reflect on a relationship that has had a profound impact on your life. What qualities made it so supportive?

Raise Your PomPoms:

- **Free**: Write thank-you notes to those who have supported you.
- **Extravagant**: Host a "gratitude dinner" for your support network.

Rally-Up Affirmation

"For every friendship, every mentor, and every loved one—Cheers to My Squad!"

Chapter 7: Stretch, Don't Stress

If you want to fly, you have to give up the things that weigh you down. – Toni Morrison

Leveling Up

Growth often happens when we're willing to step outside our comfort zones. While it can be unsettling, this 'stretch zone' is where you challenge yourself and discover new skills and perspectives.

Self-advocacy and stretching beyond my comfort zone began in a rather unexpected way. The superintendent of the school district where we lived approached me in 2012 while I was speaking at a PTA meeting. She asked me to provide customer service training for the staff. Despite never having done this for school districts specifically, my response was an emphatic "yes." My career in hotels had equipped me with extensive experience in customer service training, but this new audience required a shift in perspective and a tailored approach to the curriculum. It was a leap into the unknown, stepping into a domain I was familiar with yet had never ventured into in this specific context.

This moment marked a significant turning point for me. It was the first time I got paid for leveraging my skills and passion in a new arena, something I loved but had been hesitant to explore independently. The experience served as a powerful catalyst, igniting my entrepreneurial spirit. A decade later, this initial step paved the way for me to fully embrace my role as an entrepreneur, dedicating my efforts to helping individuals and organizations reach their potential. The decision to say "yes," despite the uncertainties and fears, was pivotal. It bolstered my confidence, reinforcing the belief that with determination and adaptability, I could achieve anything I set my mind to.

This experience taught me the value of stretching beyond comfort zones. It's a lesson I carry with me and advocate for others: **venturing into new territories, even when daunting, can lead to profound personal and professional growth.** It's in these moments of uncertainty and challenge that we often find our true capabilities and discover new perspectives. Embracing such opportunities enriches our experiences, broadening our understanding of the world and ourselves. It's a testament to the power of self-advocacy and where it can lead us, showing us that stepping out of our comfort zones not only brings victories but also enriches our view of the world in vibrant and unexpected ways.

Vibes, Voices, and Victory Moves

Taking calculated risks and cherishing small victories are indeed the dynamic duo that fuels both personal and professional evolution. Think of them as a harmonious blend of strategy and celebration, each amplifying the other's impact.

Starting with calculated risks, it's about striking a balance between audacity and prudence. It's not about diving into the unknown recklessly but charting your course with thoughtfulness and foresight. Before taking that leap, pause and reflect. Assess the landscape, weigh the potential outcomes, and consider the implications. This methodical approach not only mitigates potential pitfalls but also infuses you with a sense of empowerment. You're not merely reacting to circumstances; you're proactively making life-affirming decisions.

On the flip side, celebrating small wins nourishes the soul. Every step forward, no matter how minuscule, is a testament to your effort, determination, and growth. These moments of acknowledgment, be it a silent nod to oneself or a shared celebration with loved ones, act as fuel. They invigorate your spirit, boost your morale, and propel you forward with renewed vigor.

Research in the domain of risk management underscores the multifaceted benefits of taking informed risks. Such endeavors, when approached with discernment, can catalyze personal growth, enhance adaptability, and foster resilience. Furthermore, findings from the **Journal of Experimental Psychology** *(Russo-Netzer & Cohen, 2022)* illuminate the transformative power of stepping beyond one's comfort zone. Pushing boundaries, trying new things, and embracing challenges can accelerate skill acquisition, bolster self-confidence, and broaden horizons.

When stand at the crossroads of life, be it contemplating a bold career transition, exploring a novel hobby, or simply pushing your boundaries, remember this: **the dance between embracing risks and reveling in victories is where the magic happens.** It's this synergy that shapes you, turning challenges into opportunities and aspirations into achievements. Accept the dance, enjoy the ride, and let every risk and victory, no matter how big or small, shape your road to greatness.

Cheer Technique Breakdown

- **Skill Acquisition**: Stepping out of your comfort zone is essential for learning new skills. It's the discomfort that often catalyzes growth.
- **Personal Growth**: Taking calculated risks can lead to personal growth and a more fulfilling life.

First Day in the Cheer Spotlight:

- **Identify Comfort Zones**: Make a list of situations where you feel most comfortable.
- **Take Small Steps**: Choose one area and take a small step outside your comfort zone.

Daily Dose of Pep

1. Describe an experience where stepping out of your comfort zone led to unexpected rewards.

2. What holds you back from taking that step beyond your comfort zone?

Confessions of a Cheer Rookie

Reflect on the 'stretch zones' you've entered recently. How have they helped you grow?

Raise Your PomPoms:

- **Free**: Document how you are stepping out of your comfort zone through photos or journal entries.

- **Extravagant**: Take a class or workshop that pushes you even further out of your comfort zone.

Rally-Up Affirmation

"Beyond my comfort zone is where I grow—Stretch, don't stress!"

Chapter 8: Speak Up, Stand Out

"To say nothing is saying something. You must denounce things you are against or one might believe that you support things you really do not." - Germany Kent

Leveling Up

My mother, a trailblazer in her own right, was the first in our family to attend college. It wasn't easy, but her sacrifices paved the way for brighter futures for my sister and me. While she worked, my grandmother was our anchor, ensuring we were well-fed, educated, and instilled with a strong work ethic. Her difficult life motivated us to set higher goals for ourselves.

We were not affluent by any stretch of the imagination. In fact, we were quite the opposite. But my perception of our financial status was shaped more by our community and less by TV portrayals, which often painted a skewed picture of Black and Brown lives.

Growing up with contrasting perspectives from my grandmother and mother shaped my Gen X worldview. My child, born in the digital age of the early 2000s and having experienced global events like 9/11 and the 2020 pandemic, offers yet another generational perspective. In my family, mental health was often brushed under the carpet, with the belief that faith alone could heal all wounds. While faith is a powerful force, I believe that the divine provides us with tools and resources, including professionals, to help us navigate life's challenges. **It's a dance of action and faith, and when we do our part, the universe responds in kind.**

Using your voice is about more than just speaking; it's about making your thoughts, opinions, and feelings known in a way that can effect change, whether it's personal, professional, or societal.

My voice has always been a tool for advocacy and change, used with equal parts love and determination. In both fun and serious contexts, it has been a vehicle to champion those who are underrepresented or marginalized. My activism isn't limited to a single method; it spans from the energetic fervor of street protests to the meticulous craft of writing letters to officials. A strong commitment to oppose and alter oppressive policies is what motivates these efforts. I've never sought the path of least resistance. Instead, I've embraced the responsibility to speak out, recognizing that many are either unable or too fearful to raise their voices. My voice, therefore, becomes theirs as well, amplifying the collective call for justice and equality.

This commitment has been a constant in both my professional and personal lives. Advocating for change, especially against entrenched systems of inequality, comes with its challenges. Yet, the victories make it all worthwhile. They are reminders of the power of persistence and the impact of a single, determined voice in the chorus of change. This path of advocacy and allyship isn't just a choice; it's a core part of who I am. My pledge is to never cease using my voice for the greater good and to keep fighting for liberation and equality for all. This mission goes beyond personal fulfillment; it's about creating a legacy of change and empowerment, one voice at a time.

Vibes, Voices, and Victory Moves

Effective communication is a potent tool in the realms of activism, professional advancement, and interpersonal dynamics. It's more than just a mere exchange of words; **it's the art of conveying thoughts, emotions, and intentions with precision and passion.**

When you communicate, envision it as painting a picture with your words. Each phrase and each nuance should serve a purpose, adding depth and clarity to the canvas. It's essential to distill your message, stripping away any ambiguity or redundancy. A crisp, clear message is like a beacon, cutting through the noise and capturing attention. But clarity alone isn't enough. Infuse your communication with intent. Before you speak or write, pause and reflect. Understand the core purpose behind your words. Are you aiming to enlighten, persuade, captivate, or galvanize? This introspection ensures that your words carry weight and purpose, making them more impactful.

Delving into the academic sphere, research on activism underscores the transformative power of advocacy (Mertens, 2021). Effective communication, when harnessed in the world of activism, can catalyze societal shifts, mobilize communities, and drive tangible change (Green, 2016). It's the bridge that connects causes with supporters, turning passive listeners into active participants. Additionally, insights from public speaking journals illuminate the profound influence of articulate communication in shaping perceptions, swaying opinions, and crafting compelling narratives (Martin, 2020). The art of public speaking, when mastered, can open doors, influence stakeholders, and establish thought leadership.

As you navigate the diverse arenas of life, be it championing a social cause, leading a corporate presentation, or simply engaging in heartfelt conversations, always remember this: clarity, conciseness, and intent are the pillars of effective communication. They not only elevate your message but also forge a deep connection with your audience. By honing these skills, you're not just amplifying your voice; you're ensuring it echoes in the hearts and minds of those who hear it, leaving a lasting imprint.

Cheer Technique Breakdown

- **Advocacy and Social Change**: Speaking up is not just about individual gain; it can lead to broader social change.

- **Influencing Opinions**: Effective public speaking can change minds and inspire action.

First Day in the Cheer Spotlight:

- **Find Your Cause**: Identify issues that you're passionate about.
- **Practice Public Speaking**: Start small—perhaps with a toast at a family gathering.

Daily Dose of Pep

1. Describe a time when you used your voice to make a significant impact.
2. What challenges do you face when trying to speak up?

Confessions of a Cheer Rookie

Reflect on moments when you held back from speaking your truth. What were the circumstances, and what would you do differently now?

Raise Your PomPoms:

- **Free**: Record a video of your speech or advocacy moment and share it with close friends.
- **Extravagant**: Hire a public speaking coach for a few sessions to refine your skills.

Rally-Up Affirmation

"My voice is my power, my tool, my gift—Speak Up, Stand Out!"

____

____

____

____

____

____

Chapter 9: From Surviving to Thriving

"Don't just survive; thrive, and do it good." - Maya Angelou

Leveling Up

From a young age, watching my grandmother and mother contend with systemic inequality and financial challenges profoundly shaped my perspective. Their resilience against discrimination in a society historically unfair to Black women was both inspiring and disheartening. I grew up acutely aware that being Black and female was synonymous with facing considerable hurdles. However, **I was determined not to let this narrative define my family's future.**

The absence of my father after my parents' divorce when I was just two years old left a significant void, casting a long shadow over my future romantic relationships. Yet, the strength demonstrated by my mother and grandmother became beacons of hope, showing me that not only was survival possible, but it was also not enough for me. **I yearned to thrive and live a fulfilling life, refusing to let past challenges dictate my future.**

This resolve crystalized into a mission: to transform our legacy of survival into one of thriving. I became dedicated to changing our family's narrative, ensuring a flourishing legacy for my children and those around me. This goal became more than a personal mission; it was about reshaping the trajectory of my entire family's story.

My upbringing, filled with its unique challenges and victories, molded my responses to life. Whether dealing with an idyllic childhood or one fraught with difficulties, confronting, understanding, and working through those experiences is vital. For some, this may mean introspection; for others, seeking professional help. There's no shame in needing a guiding hand as surviving is merely getting by, but thriving is about flourishing and fully living with a sense of purpose and well-being.

My personal life, too, has been a testament to resilience and the power of self-advocacy, particularly in my journey into parenthood and discovering true partnership amid relationship challenges. Meeting someone in my late 20s who initially seemed ideal but turned out to be manipulative tested my resolve like never before. Becoming pregnant in the midst of this turbulent relationship led me to choose single motherhood over compromising my values. This difficult decision, however, paved the way to a future far brighter than I could have ever imagined.

Over the past fifteen years, love, family, and partnership have enriched my life in unexpected ways. I have been blessed with a wonderful husband who has embraced not only me but also my child, helping to raise them as his own. Together, we have built a beautiful, blended family, a testament to the unexpected paths to happiness and the profound impact of finding someone who truly understands, believes in, and supports you on your life's journey.

This part of my story highlights a crucial truth about relationships and self-advocacy: **sometimes the plans we make unravel, leading us down unforeseen paths that ultimately serve our greatest good.** It underscores the importance of adhering to our principles and self-worth through adversity and keeping an open mind to the possibilities and love that lie ahead. My narrative serves as a beacon for those navigating the often-tumultuous waters of relationships, offering hope that new beginnings are always possible, even amidst painful endings. It reaffirms that love can transform, heal, and fulfill at any stage, creating a family dynamic that is both exceptionally beautiful and deeply satisfying.

Vibes, Voices, and Victory Moves

Your mindset, like a compass, guides you through the vast landscape of life. It's the lens through which you perceive the world, influencing your reactions, decisions, and interactions. The beauty of this compass is its adaptability. By making a conscious shift from a survival-oriented mindset to one of thriving, you're not just navigating life's challenges; you're harnessing them as catalysts for growth and transformation.

Imagine the difference between merely wading through the waters of life and riding its waves with zest and zeal. This transformation in mindset doesn't just alter your trajectory; it enriches every moment, turning mundane routines into meaningful rituals and perceived setbacks into launch pads. When you operate from a place of thriving, you're not just chasing goals; you're aligning them with your deepest convictions and passions. This alignment ensures that your pursuits, be they personal or professional, resonate with your core essence, making every step of the way more rewarding.

The **World Health Organization's** research underscores the profound mental health benefits of adopting a thriving mindset (Kestel et al., 2022). Such a perspective, rooted in positivity and proactive engagement, acts as a safeguard against stress, anxiety, and burnout, enhancing overall well-being and life satisfaction. But the ripple effects of this mindset extend beyond individual well-being. Corporate wellness studies indicate that when employees transition from merely surviving to thriving, the entire organization benefits (Klinghoffer, 2023). There's a surge in productivity, creativity, and collaboration, leading to tangible economic gains and fostering a vibrant, energized workplace culture.

Charting your path, be it personal aspirations or professional ambitions, requires you to always remember this: **the power of your mindset is both**

transformational and transcendent. It's the magic wand that can reshape your reality, turning aspirations into achievements and potential into prowess. Embrace the ethos of thriving and let it illuminate every facet of your life, casting a glow of fulfillment, purpose, and joy.

Cheer Technique Breakdown

- **Mental Health**: Shifting from a survival mindset to a thriving mindset can significantly improve mental health.

- **Economic Benefits**: Organizations benefit economically when their employees are thriving, not just surviving.

First Day in the Cheer Spotlight:

- **Mindfulness**: Practice mindfulness to become aware of your thoughts and feelings.

- **Seek Professional Help**: Sometimes, shifting mindsets require professional guidance.

Daily Dose of Pep

1. Describe a situation where you felt you moved from merely surviving to thriving with certainty.
2. What are some actionable steps you can take to shift from a survival mindset to a thriving one?

Confessions of a Cheer Rookie

Reflect on any recent changes in your life that have contributed to a sense of thriving rather than just surviving.

Raise Your PomPoms:

- **Free**: Meditate or have a quiet moment to acknowledge your shift in mindset.

- **Extravagant**: Book a wellness retreat to fully embrace your new, thriving mindset.

Rally-Up Affirmation

"Surviving is my past; thriving is my future—Onward to Greatness!"

____

____

____

____

____

____

____

____

Chapter 10: Empathy: The Radical Connector

"Empathy is about finding echoes of another person in yourself." - Mohsin Hamid

Leveling Up

Radical empathy is about **deeply understanding and sharing the feelings of others, including those from backgrounds and experiences vastly different from your own**. It's empathy taken to the next level, where understanding leads to action.

The concept of radical empathy deeply resonates with my life experience, especially during a profoundly challenging time with a dear friend. She had to go through a traumatic experience after a trusted spiritual leader put her in a compromising position. When she bravely came forward, the church's initial inaction added to her trauma. Her concern extended beyond her personal hurt; she was determined to protect others in the parish from potential harm. Despite her fear, she resolved to fight for justice.

In this critical moment, I, along with two other friends, stood unwaveringly by her side. Our collective strength and determination pushed the church to take action. The process was emotionally taxing, but we persevered, leading to the removal of the perpetrator from a position of authority and the church's acknowledgment of the incident to the congregation. This outcome, while a victory, was more than just a resolution for my friend; it was a testament to the power of solidarity in the face of injustice.

This experience profoundly impacted me. It not only helped restore the self-confidence that had been eroded by my own encounters with oppressive authority structures, but it also offered a new perspective on empathy. Standing with my friend, understanding her pain, and seeing the world through her eyes transformed me. It instilled a deeper sense of purpose and responsibility. From that point on, I knew my role extended beyond my own experiences. Radical empathy became a guiding principle in my life, a commitment to stand with those carrying heavy burdens, offering support, understanding, and action. I am continuously learning to connect deeply with others' experiences, to share in their struggles, and to be an unwavering ally in their battles for justice and dignity.

Vibes, Voices, and Victory Moves

Radical empathy can be a beacon of light in a world that often feels fragmented and polarized. It's not just about feeling for another; it's about feeling with another and immersing oneself in their experiences, emotions, and perspectives. This profound connection goes beyond mere sympathy or understanding; it's about embodying another's reality, even if just momentarily M. (2023, June 30).

Active listening, the cornerstone of radical empathy, is an art in itself. It's about tuning into the unsaid, the nuances, the silent cries, and the unspoken dreams. By legitimately listening, **we're offering a gift**—a gift of presence, validation, and acknowledgment. We're communicating a powerful message: "**I see you, I hear you, and your experiences matter.**" This kind of deep, intentional listening bridges divides, fosters trust, and lays the foundation for earnest connections.

However, radical empathy is not a passive endeavor. It's dynamic and action-oriented (Burton, 2022). Once we've walked a mile in another's shoes, once we've felt their joys and sorrows, it compels us to act. Whether it's advocating for societal change, offering support, or simply being a shoulder to lean on, radical empathy drives us to make a tangible difference. **It's about transforming understanding into action and compassion into change.**

Insights from the **Stanford Social Innovation Review** (Follow the Fool (SSIR), n.d.) and the **Journal of Patient Experience** (Riess, 2017) illuminate the myriad societal benefits of radical empathy. Such an approach, when embraced collectively, can mitigate biases, combat discrimination, and foster inclusivity. It acts as a catalyst for societal transformation, promoting mental well-being, reducing prejudices, and weaving a tapestry of unity and understanding.

Throughout the diverse arenas of life, be they personal interactions, professional endeavors, or societal engagements, **always remember this**: radical empathy is not just a philosophy; it's a movement. It's the key to unlocking a world where understanding transcends barriers, compassion drives action, and every individual feels seen, heard, and valued. By embracing and championing radical empathy, we're not just enhancing individual lives; we're sculpting a world that's more harmonious, inclusive, and profoundly connected.

Cheer Technique Breakdown

- **Psychological Benefits**: Empathy can lead to better mental health as it helps you connect with others on a deeper level.
- **Societal Impact**: Radical empathy can lead to more inclusive communities and even policy changes.

First Day in the Cheer Spotlight:

- **Active Listening**: Make a conscious effort to listen more than you speak.
- **Be Open**: Don't be quick to judge; try to understand where the other person is coming from.

Daily Dose of Pep

1. Describe a situation where you practiced radical empathy. What was the outcome?

2. What challenges do you face when trying to practice radical empathy?

Confessions of a Cheer Rookie

Reflect on how your understanding of empathy has evolved over time. Are there ways you could practice more radical empathy in your life?

Raise Your PomPoms:

- **Free**: Have a heartfelt conversation with someone you've helped or who has helped you.

- **Extravagant**: Sponsor someone in need as a way to extend your empathy even further.

Rally-Up Affirmation

"I see you, I hear you, and I stand by you—empathy to action!"

Chapter 11: Rest is Revolutionary

"You have enough. You do enough. You are enough. Relax." – Unknown

Leveling Up

In a society that often glorifies busyness and overwork, taking time to rest is an act of resistance. Rest is not just physical; it's also emotional and mental. It's about giving yourself permission to pause, reflect, and recharge.

Growing up in an era dominated by the 'rise and grind' mentality profoundly shaped my approach to life and work. This hustle culture, with its relentless emphasis on success and competition, drove me to constantly push my limits. It was a race where the finish line kept moving further away. Amidst this pursuit of achievement and recognition, I lost sight of the essentials: my physical health, mental well-being, and the simple joys of life. My focus was so fixated on outperforming others and amassing accolades that I ignored the signals my body and mind were sending. Happiness became elusive; each accomplishment was merely a jump-off to the next, leaving no room for self-celebration or contentment.

This perpetual chase led to a profound realization: **true success isn't about relentless work or constant comparison with others. It's about understanding and honoring oneself.** I learned that rest is not just important; it's revolutionary. Stepping away from the unyielding demands of hustle culture, I embraced a new philosophy. Life isn't just about work; it's about balance, or rather, a harmonious integration of work and rest. This shift in perspective has been enlightening, especially in my later life. I've had to unlearn and relearn many misguided comparisons, recognizing that the only meaningful ones are making sure who I am today is better than I was yesterday and only a fraction of who I aspire to be tomorrow.

This personal transformation has not only been beneficial for me but has also been instrumental in guiding others. By sharing my experience, I help people understand the significance of rest, self-care, and self-compassion. It's about shifting the narrative from constant competition to personal growth and well-being. This newfound wisdom is a message I am passionate about conveying: that in a world obsessed with constant doing, sometimes the most powerful action is to pause, reflect, and simply be. It's a lesson in finding fulfillment not just through achievements but through a balanced, introspective, and self-aware approach to life.

Vibes, Voices, and Victory Moves

Taking care of oneself is a holistic endeavor, encompassing not just the physical but the emotional, mental, and even spiritual dimensions of our being. It's about nurturing the entirety of who we are, ensuring that every facet is attended to and balanced.

Setting boundaries is fundamental for creating protective barriers that can safeguard our mental and emotional space (Lmft, 2023). It's about understanding our limits, recognizing when we're stretched too thin, and having the courage to assertively communicate our needs. Saying 'no' isn't a sign of weakness; it's an assertion of self-awareness and self-respect. It's about acknowledging that while we have the capacity to do many things, we owe it to ourselves to do them well without compromising our well-being.

The age-old adage "quality over quantity" rings especially true here. Instead of being caught in the relentless cycle of doing more, it's about doing better. It's about immersing oneself fully in tasks, ensuring that each endeavor is infused with care, attention, and excellence. But to achieve this level of quality, rest and rejuvenation are critical. Just as a car needs regular refueling to run efficiently, our minds and bodies need regular breaks to function optimally.

The **World Health Organization (WHO)** offer compelling insights into the perils of overworking (Chappell, 2021). The repercussions of neglecting self-care and boundaries extend beyond mere fatigue. It can manifest as chronic stress, anxiety, severe health conditions, and even death. Conversely, setting boundaries, prioritizing rest, and managing time effectively can elevate our productivity, creativity, and overall well-being.

In the contemporary landscape, especially in the wake of the COVID-19 pandemic, the lines between work and personal life have blurred for many. The challenge of maintaining a work-life balance has intensified, with burnout lurking ominously in the shadows. This calls for a collective shift in organizational cultures. Employers need to champion a culture of well-being, emphasizing the importance of balance, flexibility, and mental health.

Offering perks that cater to mental well-being, fostering a supportive work environment, and leading by example are pivotal. After all, a team that feels valued, supported, and rested is one that thrives, innovates, and excels.

While juggling duties and objectives, keep in mind that your well-being is crucial. It's the foundation upon which all else is built. Prioritize yourself, set clear boundaries, and embrace the power of rest. By doing so, you're not just ensuring your own flourishing but also setting a powerful example for those around you. Embrace self-care as a non-negotiable and watch how it transforms every facet of your life, infusing it with joy, balance, and fulfillment.

Cheer Technique Breakdown

- **Health Effects**: Overworking can lead to both physical and mental health issues, including burnout.

- **Importance of Rest**: Taking time to rest and recharge is crucial for long-term productivity and well-being.

First Day in the Cheer Spotlight:

- **Set Boundaries**: Make it clear when you're "off the clock."
- **Prioritize Self-Care**: Schedule regular breaks and stick to them.

Daily Dose of Pep

1. Describe a time when you consciously chose rest over work. What impact did it have on your well-being?
2. How can you incorporate more restful moments into your daily routine?

Confessions of a Cheer Rookie

Reflect on your relationship with rest. Do you find it challenging to take breaks? If so, why?

Raise Your PomPoms:

- **Free**: Take a full day off to do absolutely nothing.
- **Extravagant**: Book a spa day or weekend to fully recharge.

Rally-Up Affirmation

- "Rest is not a luxury; it's a necessity. Pause, breathe, and recharge!"

____

____

____

____

Time to Find Your Own Biggest Cheerleader

And so, we arrive at the conclusion of our shared voyage within these pages, yet we stand on the brink of countless new beginnings. My fervent hope is that if there's one enduring message you carry from this book, it's the recognition of your inherent power. You are indeed your own most ardent cheerleader. Within you lies the strength to realize your dreams, surmount any challenge, and carve out a life rich with meaning and joy.

As you prepare to step forward, I offer you these three pivotal keys to unlocking the vast potential within you:

1. **Believe in Yourself**: Trust in your abilities and worth. This belief lays the foundation for all your future successes.

2. **Ask for What You Want**: Remember, silence rarely brings opportunity. Articulate your desire, and let the universe hear you.

3. **Seek Community Support**: Our lives and experiences are enriched and made possible through the strength of community. You are not alone; draw upon the collective strength around you.

As this book closes, imagine it as the closing of one chapter and the exciting beginning of another in the grand narrative of your life. **You are the author of your story. What will your next sentence be? What adventures, learnings, and growth await you in the chapters to come?**

Thank you for allowing me to share my truths with you. Now, it's time for you to step out and be your own biggest cheerleader. The world awaits your unique contributions, so go ahead and make your mark!

Love Letter to Myself: My Journey to ______________

Feel free to print this out, fill in the blanks, and keep it somewhere special. Whenever you need a boost of motivation or a reminder of how far you've come, this letter will be here to uplift you.

Dear Me,

Wow, what a journey it's been! I remember when I first started the chapter on ________________________ [***Chapter Title***], feeling ________________________ [***Emotion***]. But look at me now; I've ________________________ [***Achievement***].

In my quest for ________________________ [***Goal***], I've learned the importance of ________________________ [***Lesson from Chapter***]. I'm so proud of myself for ________________________ [***Specific Action You Took***]. It wasn't easy, but I did it, and that's worth celebrating.

I've also become a better ________________________ [***Role You Play in Life, e.g., Leader, Ally, Friend***] by embracing ____________________ [***Concept, e.g., Allyship, Emotional Intelligence***]. This has not only helped me but also positively impacted ________________________ [***People or Community You've Helped***].

One of the most transformative moments was when I ________________________ ***[Moment of Realization or Achievement***]. It made me feel ________________________ [***Positive Emotion***], and I knew then that I was on the right path.

I want to give a special shoutout to ________________________ [***Name or Description of Supportive People***], who have been my rock(s) through this journey. Your support has been invaluable, and I couldn't have done it without you.

As I raise my pompoms to celebrate, I'm treating myself to ________________________ [***Your "Raise Your PomPoms" Celebration***]. I've earned it!

Looking ahead, I'm excited to ________________________ [***Next Step or Goal***]. I know there will be challenges, but I'm ready to face them with ________________________ [***Quality or Skill You've Gained***].

So here's to me, for being ____________________________ [***3 Adjectives That Describe You Now***]. I can't wait to see where this journey takes me next.

With all the love and pompoms,

________________________ [***Your Name***]

Acknowledgements

Writing this book has been extraordinary. It has transformed me in ways I could have never imagined. The support and love I've received along this path have been nothing short of incredible. I am deeply grateful for every ounce of encouragement and every gesture of support that lifted me during moments of doubt and fueled my passion during bursts of inspiration.

First and foremost, I am grateful to my spouse, Brian. You have been my most fierce advocate and my unwavering rock. Your steady support has given me a strong foundation of love and faith.

To my children, Aujolie and Jason, you embody creativity and compassion in their purest forms. Your presence in my life is a daily inspiration, constantly motivating me to strive for better and to be a better version of myself.

My mother, Joyce, your resilience and grace have been my guiding lights, illuminating my path with wisdom and love. And to my sister, Audra, the loyalty and encouragement you have shown me are treasures I hold close to my heart.

I want to express my sincere gratitude to my group of pals. Throughout every stage of my life, your everlasting faith in me and your steadfast support have been my greatest sources of strength.

This book is also the culmination of 35 years of work in emotional intelligence, relationship-building, and inclusive leadership. I owe a debt of gratitude to the numerous mentors, colleagues, and communities who have given their time, talent, and treasure to me. It is on the shoulders of these giants that I stand.

Finally, to you, the reader, who chose to pick up this book. Your commitment to your personal growth and well-being is commendable. I sincerely hope that the insights shared here enrich your life as much as they have enriched mine in writing.

Thank you, from the bottom of my heart, for honoring me in this way!

Index

Chappell, B. (2021, May 17). *Overwork Killed More Than 745,000 People In A Year, WHO Study Finds*. NPR. https://www.npr.org/2021/05/17/997462169/thousands-of-people-are-dying-from-working-long-hours-a-new-who-study-finds

Lmft, M. C. B. B. (2023, September 14). *How to Set Healthy Boundaries With Anyone*. Verywell Health. https://www.verywellhealth.com/setting-boundaries-5208802

Follow the Fool (SSIR). (n.d.). (C) 2005-2024. https://doi.org/10.48558/B5NZ-W482

Riess, H. (2017, May 9). *The Science of Empathy*. Journal of Patient Experience. https://doi.org/10.1177/2374373517699267

Burton, N. (2022, May 16). *"Radical Empathy" Is the Only Thing That Can Save the World - Here's How*. Goalcast. https://www.goalcast.com/radical-empathy/

M. (2023, June 30). *How to Cultivate Compassion with Radical Empathy - Positive Inner Growth*. Positive Inner Growth. https://positiveinnergrowth.com/radical-empathy/#:~:text=Radical%20empathy%2C%20as%20the%20term%20suggests%2C%20is%20about,approach%20situations%20with%20an%20open%20mind%20and%20heart.

Klinghoffer, D. (2023, February 6). *Why Microsoft Measures Employee Thriving, Not Engagement*. Harvard Business Review. https://hbr.org/2022/06/why-microsoft-measures-employee-thriving-not-engagement

Kestel, D., Lewis, S., Freeman, M., Chisholm, D., Gascoigne Siegl, O., & van Ommeren, M. (2022, October 1). A world report on the transformation needed in mental health care. *Bulletin of the World Health Organization*, *100*(10), 583–583. https://doi.org/10.2471/blt.22.289123

Martin, J. (2020, July 6). Rhetoric, discourse and the hermeneutics of public speech. *Politics*, *42*(2), 170–184. https://doi.org/10.1177/0263395720933779

Green, D. (2016, October 27). The Power of Advocacy. *How Change Happens*, 212–232. https://doi.org/10.1093/acprof:oso/9780198785392.003.0014

Mertens, D. M. (2021, January). Transformative Research Methods to Increase Social Impact for Vulnerable Groups and Cultural Minorities.

International Journal of Qualitative Methods, *20*, 160940692110515. https://doi.org/10.1177/16094069211051563

Russo-Netzer, P., & Cohen, G. L. (2022, May 15). 'If you're uncomfortable, go outside your comfort zone': A novel behavioral 'stretch' intervention supports the well-being of unhappy people. *The Journal of Positive Psychology*, *18*(3), 394–410. https://doi.org/10.1080/17439760.2022.2036794

Casanova, B. E. C., Felix, C. A. C., Balingit, N. D. Z., de Vera, A. M. F., Briones, M. D. M., & Aruta, J. J. B. R. (2022, August 5). Social support and bidimensional mental health among primary-level teachers during COVID-19 crisis. *International Journal of School & Educational Psychology*, *11*(3), 245–258.

https://doi.org/10.1080/21683603.2022.2105998

Ortiz-Ospina, E., & Roser, M. (2024, March 20). *Happiness and Life Satisfaction*. Our World in Data. https://ourworldindata.org/happiness-and-life-satisfaction

Wilson, C. R. (2024, February 28). *Healthy Coping Mechanisms: 9 Adaptive Strategies to Try*. PositivePsychology.com. https://positivepsychology.com/healthy-coping-mechanisms/

Emotional Intelligence (EQ): Components and Examples. (2024, January 29). Simply Psychology. https://www.simplypsychology.org/emotional-intelligence.html

Schaefer, E. (2024, February 20). *Empathy in Dialogue: Mastering Non-Violent Communication — Agile*

Ideation. Agile Ideation. https://agile-ideation.com/blog/2024/2/20/empathy-in-dialogue-mastering-non-violent-communication#:~:text=Empathy%20is%20the%20linchpin%20of%20NVC.%20It%20involves,trust%2C%20allowing%20for%20more%20authentic%20and%20constructive%20dialogues.

Emotion Science. (n.d.). Child Study Center. https://medicine.yale.edu/childstudy/services/community-and-schools-programs/center-for-emotional-intelligence/research/emotion-science/

Striking findings from 2022 | Pew Research Center. (2022, December 15). Pew Research Center. https://www.pewresearch.org/short-reads/2022/12/13/striking-findings-from-2022/

Hunt, D. V., Yee, L., Prince, S., & Dixon-Fyle, S. (2018, January 18). *Delivering through diversity*.

McKinsey & Company.

https://www.mckinsey.com/capabilities/people-and-organizational-performance/our-insights/delivering-through-diversity

About the Author

Lachandra B. Baker is a distinguished leader, advocate, and visionary whose life and career have been dedicated to fostering inclusivity, engagement, and personal empowerment. She is the founder and lead consultant at LBB Edutainment, a consultancy renowned for its expertise in employee engagement, communication, culture, and diversity, equity, inclusion, and belonging (DEIB). With over thirty-five years of professional experience spanning multiple sectors including hospitality, finance, non-profit, technology, and healthcare, Lachandra has become a pivotal figure in shaping productive and inclusive corporate cultures.

Lachandra holds a bachelor's degree in Hospitality Management and Communications from Central Washington University and an MBA with a specialization in Marketing from the University of the Southwest. She has also earned prestigious certifications in Diversity,

Equity, and Inclusion from Cornell University, highlighting her commitment to advancing these crucial areas in both professional and community settings.

Throughout her career, Lachandra has been recognized for her leadership and impact. She was named a 2021 Columbus Future50 leader, a 2022 WELD Women WELDing the Way calendar honoree, and a 2023 Columbus Delegate for the Harvard University Young American Leaders program. Her work has not only garnered accolades but has also made significant improvements in company cultures and employee engagement across various organizations.

Beyond her professional endeavors, Lachandra is deeply involved in her community. She serves on several boards including The Women's Fund of Central Ohio, Leadership Columbus, and Small Biz Cares, and contributes to advisory boards with Cinema Columbus and Creative Mornings Columbus. Her activism extends to advocating for voting rights, affordable housing, and civic engagement, emphasizing her dedication to creating a fairer and more equitable society.

Lachandra is also a gifted communicator and frequent TEDx speaker and performer, where she shares her insights on leadership, empowerment, and community involvement. Her compelling presentations have inspired many to take active roles in their personal and professional lives, advocating for change and fostering environments where everyone can thrive.

In her free time, Lachandra enjoys exploring new cultures, indulging in great food, and engaging in creative projects with her family. Her life's work and leisure activities reflect her belief in the power of personal development, community involvement, and the joy of living a fully engaged life.

Lachandra B. Baker's journey is a testament to the power of resilience, leadership, and the relentless pursuit of inclusivity. Through her writing, speaking, and consulting, she continues to inspire and empower individuals and organizations to embrace their true potential and advocate for transformative change.

www.ingramcontent.com/pod-product-compliance
Lightning Source LLC
LaVergne TN
LVHW050551160826
845677LV00011B/2263

* 9 7 9 8 8 9 3 7 2 0 0 6 8 *